Texas Longhorns IQ: The Ultimate Test of True Fandom

Richard Brown

IQ Series books are the trademark of Black Mesa Publishing, LLC.

Cataloging-in-Publication Data is available from the Library of Congress.

ISBN: 978-0-9837922-2-2
First edition, first printing

Cover photo courtesy of Marty De Los Santos.

Black Mesa Publishing, LLC
Florida
David Horne and Marc CB Maxwell
Black.Mesa.Publishing@gmail.com

Texas Longhorns Football

"Football doesn't build character – it eliminates the weak ones."
– Darrell Royal

Introduction

THE UNIVERSITY OF TEXAS football program is a national power. No ifs, buts or doubts about it. It has become one of the elite.

The facilities, coaches, players, administrative support and fans are among the finest anywhere. But it's been a long journey – it didn't happen overnight. It was a gradual process with ups and downs. For sure, the journey has included a number of outstanding players and coaches.

The intent of this book is to refresh and rekindle your positive memories of some of the finest players and the coaches who have played such a significant role in helping make the University of Texas football program one of the finest in the country.

Longhorn Nation, sit back. Enjoy. Read this IQ book by yourself or with friends and family around the trivia table.

This is for Texas football fans everywhere around the country.

It's great to be a Longhorn!

"You don't belong in a game like this if you don't feel good about yourself and walk with a swagger. If you think you can be stopped, this isn't the place for you."
— Mack Brown

Texas Longhorns IQ

QUESTION 1: The Longhorns won their first National Championship in what year?
   a) 1962
   b) 1963
   c) 1968
   d) 1969

QUESTION 2: Who did the Longhorns defeat for their second National Championship?
   a) UCLA
   b) Notre Dame
   c) Ohio State
   d) Oklahoma

QUESTION 3: The Longhorns won their third National Championship after defeating these two teams, one for the SWC Championship and the other in the Cotton Bowl for the UPI (United Press International) National Championship.
   a) Baylor and Oklahoma
   b) Texas Tech and Navy
   c) Arkansas and Notre Dame
   d) Texas A&M and Ohio State

QUESTION 4: The Longhorns went undefeated with a 13-0 record during this National Championship year. Which year was it?
   a) 1963
   b) 1969
   c) 1970
   d) 2005

QUESTION 5: In which year did the Longhorns lose their final game of the season, a Cotton Bowl defeat, but were still

recognized as the National Champion by the *United Press International.*
  a) 1967
  b) 1968
  c) 1969
  d) 1970

QUESTION 6: When did the Longhorns win their first *official* SWC Championship?
  a) 1916
  b) 1917
  c) 1943
  d) 1945

QUESTION 7: Texas holds the record for most SWC Championships with how many titles?
  a) 24
  b) 25
  c) 26
  d) 27

QUESTION 8: Texas holds the record for most consecutive SWC Championships with how many titles?
  a) 4
  b) 5
  c) 6
  d) 7

QUESTION 9: In what year did UT win its last SWC title?
  a) 1993
  b) 1994
  c) 1995
  d) 1996

QUESTION 10: How many times (seasons) did the Longhorns

go undefeated in SWC play?
- a) 15
- b) 16
- c) 17
- d) 18

QUESTION 11: This Memorable Bowl game occurred when the Longhorns made their first appearance in a Rose Bowl, and defeated their opponent, 38-37. Who did the Longhorns play?
- a) Wisconsin
- b) USC
- c) Penn State
- d) Michigan

QUESTION 12: This Memorable Bowl game was the Longhorns first bowl win. The Longhorns defeated Georgia Tech, 14-7, in 1943. Name this major bowl.
- a) Orange Bowl
- b) Rose Bowl
- c) Sugar Bowl
- d) Cotton Bowl

QUESTION 13: Texas has played in the Cotton Bowl 22 times. What Bowl game have the Longhorns played in 6 times?
- a) Bluebonnet Bowl
- b) Holiday Bowl
- c) Sugar Bowl
- d) Sun Bowl

QUESTION 14: In this Memorable Bowl game Texas slipped by this Big Ten opponent, 24-21. It was the last time UT played a Big Ten team in a Bowl game before the Big Ten became a 12 team Conference. What Big Ten opponent did the Longhorns whip?
- a) Michigan
- b) Ohio State

c) Michigan State
d) Illinois

QUESTION 15: The Longhorns have played in the Gator Bowl only one time? Who was its opponent?
a) Alabama
b) Auburn
c) Florida
d) Ole Miss

QUESTION 16: Inaugural Big 12 Championship. A three touchdown underdog, Texas stunned the third ranked team in the nation 37-27 on December 7, 1996. Priest Holmes ran for 120 yards and 3 TDs. Who did UT beat?
a) Colorado
b) Kansas State
c) Nebraska
d) Missouri

QUESTION 17: Undefeated, third-ranked Houston led by Heisman Trophy candidate David Klingler, arrived in Austin on November 10, 1990. In the previous three meetings, Houston had run up 173 points (57.7 per game) on the Longhorns in winning three consecutive games. Not in 1990. The UT defense grounded the Cougars. Texas intercepted Klingler four times and held the Cougars to 81 yards on 31 plays when the game was being decided in the second and third quarters. What was the margin of victory for the Longhorns?
a) 21 points
b) 28 points
c) 35 points
d) 42 points

QUESTION 18: Hunter Lawrence nailed a 46 yard field goal as time expired to give Texas a 13-12 victory over Nebraska in 2009 Big 12 Conference Championship. Where did this game take place?

a) Kansas City, Missouri
b) Cowboys Stadium – Dallas, Texas
c) Cotton Bowl – Dallas, Texas
d) Lincoln, Nebraska

QUESTION 19: On October 11, 2008, UT beat Oklahoma 45-35. This was the first time since 1963 that a Longhorns team beat a #1 ranked team during the regular season. What was UT's rank heading into this Red River Rivalry matchup?
a) 3
b) 4
c) 5
d) 6

QUESTION 20: On October 14, 1989, a freshman Quarterback led the Longhorns past the OU Sooners, 28-24. This QB went on to beat the Oklahoma Sooners all four times during his career, making him the first UT QB to do so. Who was this player?
a) Colt McCoy
b) Peter Gardere
c) Major Applewhite
d) Rick McIvor

QUESTION 21: Going into the 2011 season, how many National television appearances have the Longhorns had?
a) 199
b) 200
c) 210
d) 211

QUESTION 22: Going in to the 2011 season, how many regional television appearances have the Longhorns had?
a) 177
b) 178
c) 181
d) 182

QUESTION 23: In this year the Longhorns made their first television appearances vs. the Oklahoma Sooners and the TCU Horned Frogs. What year was it?
a)   1946
b)   1947
c)   1948
d)   1949

QUESTION 24: In 2010, UT played their first televised game of the season vs. what team?
a) Wyoming
b) Rice
c) UCLA
d) Texas Tech

QUESTION 25: Going in to the 2011 season, how many televised games have UT won?
a) 240
b) 259
c) 263
d) 270

QUESTION 26: In what year did coach Clyde Littlefield order "Burnt" orange uniforms instead of the original "bright" orange the Longhorns originally wore?
a) 1926
b) 1927
c) 1928
d) 1929

QUESTION 27: Because the darker orange dye was too expensive during the Great Depression, UT had to resort back to the bright orange uniforms until what coach changed them back to burnt orange... once again?
a) Mack Brown
b) Dana Bible

c) Blair Cherry
d) Darrell Royal

QUESTION 28: What is the last word to the song, "The Eyes of Texas"?
a) Texas
b) Day
c) Horn
d) University

QUESTION 29: In what year did the "Hook 'em Horns" hand signal start?
a) 1955
b) 1956
c) 1957
d) 1958

QUESTION 30: What is the name of the cannon that resides in the south end zone area at home football games?
a) Blaze
b) Smokey
c) Fire
d) Fight

QUESTION 31: Entering the 2009 season, what was Darrell K Royal – Texas Memorial Stadium's capacity?
a) 99,679
b) 100,065
c) 100,119
d) 101,103

QUESTION 32: How much did it cost to put in the Prostar Video Board, which is 55 feet high by 134 feet wide?
a) $6 million
b) $7 million
c) $8 million
d) $9 million

QUESTION 33: Against what team did UT record its largest crowd at Darrell K Royal – Texas Memorial Stadium; 101,437 faithful Longhorns?
   a) UTEP
   b) Texas A&M
   c) Oklahoma State
   d) UCLA

QUESTION 34: Through the 2010 season, how many overall home wins does UT have?
   a) 490
   b) 491
   c) 492
   d) 493

QUESTION 35: In what year did UT put in "artificial turf" for the first time?
   a) 1968
   b) 1969
   c) 1970
   d) 1971

QUESTION 36: When was the last time Texas played the Deaf School?
   a) 1903
   b) 1905
   c) 1907
   d) 1909

QUESTION 37: Through the 2010 season, how many wins have the Longhorns recorded over rival Oklahoma?
   a) 57
   b) 58
   c) 59
   d) 60

QUESTION 38: How many recorded wins does UT have over Austin YMCA?
- a) 3
- b) 4
- c) 5
- d) 6

QUESTION 39: How many overall wins does Texas have vs. Texas A&M through the 2010 season?
- a) 75
- b) 76
- c) 77
- d) 78

QUESTION 40: In what year did the Texas – Texas Tech rivalry begin?
- a) 1926
- b) 1927
- c) 1928
- d) 1929

QUESTION 41: Who holds the single season rushing record at UT with 2,124 yards?
- a) Ricky Williams
- b) Cedric Benson
- c) Vince Young
- d) Earl Campbell

QUESTION 42: What Longhorn holds the career rushing record with 6,279 yards?
- a) Ricky Williams
- b) Cedric Benson
- c) Vince Young
- d) Earl Campbell

QUESTION 43: What Longhorn has the most 100 yard rushing

games in a single season at 11?
 a) Ricky Williams
 b) Cedric Benson
 c) Vince Young
 d) Earl Campbell

QUESTION 44: In what year did Len Barrell become the first Longhorn to rush for over 100 yards in a game?
 a) 1912
 b) 1913
 c) 1914
 d) 1915

QUESTION 45: What Longhorn holds the longest run in UT history with a 96 yard dash vs. TCU?
 a) Ricky Williams
 b) Chris Gilbert
 c) Terry Orr
 d) Jamaal Charles

QUESTION 46: What was R.D. Wentworth's (UT's first Head Coach) salary in 1894.
 a) $250
 b) $325
 c) $450
 d) $525

QUESTION 47: Who is the only Longhorn coach to go undefeated during his full tenure at UT?
 a) Coach Frank Crawford
 b) Coach Harry Robinson
 c) Coach Maurice Clarke
 d) Coach J.B. Hart

QUESTION 48: How many UT Head Coaches have there been through the 2010 season?

a) 24
b) 26
c) 28
d) 30

QUESTION 49: In what year did Mack Brown win the Bobby Dodd National Coach of the Year award?
a) 2005
b) 2006
c) 2007
d) 2008

QUESTION 50: What coach never had a losing season at UT during his 20 years in Austin?
a) Coach Fred Akers
b) Coach Darrell Royal
c) Coach Mack Brown
d) Coach Blair Cherry

QUESTION 51: In what year did Earl Campbell win the Heisman Trophy?
a) 1976
b) 1977
c) 1978
d) 1979

QUESTION 52: Who is the only player in UT history to snag the Butkus Award, for the nation's best collegiate linebacker?
a) Brian Orakpo
b) Tony Degrate
c) Kenneth Sims
d) Derrick Johnson

QUESTION 53: Who is the only player in Longhorns history to win the Doak Walker Award, twice?
a) Earl Campbell
b) Cedric Benson

c) Ricky Williams
d) Colt McCoy

"I don't know. Never had one."
— Darrell K. Royal, to Mack Brown on how to coach a team after a losing season

---

QUESTION 54: Which of these players did NOT win the prestigious Maxwell Award, signifying the nation's premiere college football player?
a) Tommy Nobis
b) Vince Young
c) Colt McCoy
d) Dallas Griffin

QUESTION 55: Who is the only running back in UT history to win the Davey O'Brien National Quarterback Award?
a) Earl Campbell
b) Cedric Benson
c) Ricky Williams
d) Colt McCoy

QUESTION 56: The Jim Thorpe Award was created in 1986 and is given to the nation's best defensive back. What UT player was the first recipient of the national honor?
a) Aaron Ross
b) Michael Huff
c) Tommy Nobis
d) Scott Appleton

QUESTION 57: The Outland Trophy honors the nation's most outstanding interior lineman. Who was the first player in UT history to win the award?
a) Aaron Ross
b) Michael Huff
c) Tommy Nobis
d) Scott Appleton

QUESTION 58: Who is the only player in Longhorn history to win The Walter Camp Football Foundation Player of the Year award, twice?
a) Earl Campbell
b) Cedric Benson
c) Ricky Williams
d) Colt McCoy

QUESTION 59: Vince Young and Colt McCoy have both won the Manning Award. Prior to what season was the Manning Award created?
a) 2003
b) 2004
c) 2005
d) 2006

QUESTION 60: What UT quarterback won the Johnny Unitas Golden Arm Award?
a) Chris Simms
b) Vince Young
c) Colt McCoy
d) Major Applewhite

QUESTION 61: In the Longhorns locker room, how many personalized eight-foot tall lockers are there?
a) 75
b) 100
c) 125
d) 150

QUESTION 62: How large is the Bryan and Deborah Stolle Academic Center, where the Longhorns football team can prepare for success in the classroom?
a) 2,000 square feet
b) 2,250 square feet
c) 2,500 square feet
d) 2,750 square feet

QUESTION 63: How much did it cost to build UT's indoor practice facility?
a) $3 million
b) $4 million
c) $5 million
d) $6 million

QUESTION 64: Each year UT holds an annual Torchlight Parade to prepare for a rival opponent. What opponent are they preparing for?
a) Texas Tech
b) Texas A&M
c) Baylor
d) University of Oklahoma

QUESTION 65: What is displayed on the UT Tower when the Football team wins a National title?
a) A Longhorn
b) The No. 1
c) A Lone Star
d) The Texas Flag

QUESTION 66: Who sponsored the "Tailgater of the Game" competition at UT in 2010?
a) AT&T
b) H-E-B
c) Dell
d) Lone Star Beer

QUESTION 67: What item is not prohibited at Longhorns games?
a) Strollers
b) Banners
c) Umbrellas
d) Point and Shoot Cameras

QUESTION 68: When was the last and only time the Longhorns played the University of Arizona?
a) 1912
b) 1925
c) 1938
d) 1950

QUESTION 69: Which Military Installation did the Longhorns play and beat?
a) Corpus Christi Naval Air Station
b) Fort Hood
c) Fort Bliss
d) Corpus Christi Army Depot

QUESTION 70: How many players from UT with a last name starting with a Z, played in the NFL as of 2010?
a) 0
b) 1
c) 2
d) 3

QUESTION 71: On November 28, 2009 Marquise Goodwin set a UT record for longest Kickoff return for a touchdown. How long was his run?
a) 94 yards
b) 95 yards
c) 96 yards
d) 97 yards

QUESTION 72: Which UT quarterback has recorded more victories as a starting quarterback?
a) Vince Young
b) Bobby Layne
c) Colt McCoy
d) James Street

QUESTION 73: Which Longhorn quarterback started 41 games?
a) Colt McCoy
b) Peter Gardere
c) James Brown
d) Bret Stafford

QUESTION 74: Which UT quarterback threw a record 156 straight passes without throwing an interception?
a) Major Applewhite
b) Chris Simms
c) James Brown
d) Colt McCoy

QUESTION 75: Athlon Sports' 2011 preseason poll ranked Texas where?
a) 20th
b) 22nd
c) 24th
d) 26th

QUESTION 76: Who was the first quarterback in NCAA history to rush for over 1,000 yards and pass for over 3,000 yards in the same season?
a) Major Applewhite
b) Chris Simms
c) Vince Young
d) Colt McCoy

QUESTION 77: Who holds the career scoring record at UT with 452 points?

a) Ricky Williams
b) Cedric Benson
c) Earl Campbell
d) Hunter Lawrence

QUESTION 78: What place-kicker holds the career scoring record for kickers with 358 points?
a) Ryan Bailey
b) Kris Stockton
c) Phil Dawson
d) Dusty Mangum

QUESTION 79: Which UT team set a school record for most yards tallied with 6,657 yards?
a) 2003 squad
b) 2005 squad
c) 2007 squad
d) 2009 squad

QUESTION 80: What Longhorn kicker holds the UT record for most extra point attempts in a season with 77 tries?
a) David Pino
b) Dusty Magnum
c) Billy Schott
d) Kris Stockton

QUESTION 81: In 1977, this kicker set a UT record for the longest field made at 67 yards. What is his name?
a) David Pino
b) Russell Erxleben
c) Billy Schott
d) Jeff ward

QUESTION 82: Through his career from 1976-79, Johnnie Johnson set a Longhorns record for most punt returns. How

many punts returns did Johnson attempt?
   a) 111
   b) 112
   c) 113
   d) 114

QUESTION 83: Who was UT's opponent in the 1948 Sugar Bowl, which the Longhorns won 27-7?
   a) LSU
   b) Alabama
   c) Auburn
   d) Ole Miss

QUESTION 84: Who did the Longhorns play during their first appearance in the Orange Bowl?
   a) Florida
   b) Alabama
   c) Georgia
   d) Ole Miss

QUESTION 85: Through the 2010 season, who is the only team with more appearances in bowl games?
   a) USC
   b) Nebraska
   c) Alabama
   d) Tennessee

QUESTION 86: In 1917, UT had only one player receive All-Conference honors. Who was this player?
   a) Pig Dittmar
   b) Maxey Hart
   c) Rip Lang
   d) Dewey Bradford

QUESTION 87: Who was the 2008 Big 12 conference Defensive Player of the Year?

a) Earl Thomas
b) Brian Orakpo
c) Emanuel Acho
d) Sam Acho

QUESTION 88: What player did NOT win the AT&T/ABC Sports Player of the Year award?
a) Cedric Benson
b) Vince Young
c) Ricky Williams
d) Colt McCoy

QUESTION 89: In what Texas town was Earl Campbell born?
a) Bishop
b) Sinton
c) Tyler
d) Laredo

QUESTION 90: In what year did Earl Campbell win NFL Rookie of the Year honors?
a) 1976
b) 1977
c) 1978
d) 1979

QUESTION 91: Prior to the 2005 National Championship season, when was the last time the Longhorns went undefeated?
a) 1969
b) 1972
c) 1975
d) 1978

QUESTION 92: After the Longhorns won their 4th National Title, how many total wins did the Longhorns have in the history of

their program?
   a) 650
   b) 700
   c) 750
   d) 800

QUESTION 93: Prior to beating USC in the 2005 National Title Game, when was the last time a UT team beat a #1 ranked opponent (Oklahoma)?
   a) 1953
   b) 1963
   c) 1973
   d) 1983

QUESTION 94: During the Longhorns 1963 title run, how many of their opponents were non Texas schools?
   a) 3
   b) 4
   c) 5
   d) 6

QUESTION 95: How many people were in attendance to watch the #1 Longhorns beat the #9 Notre Dame Fighting Irish in the Cotton Bowl during the 1969 title season?
   a) 53,000
   b) 63,000
   c) 73,000
   d) 83,000

QUESTION 96: Familiar scene... How many people were in attendance to watch the #1 Longhorns beat the #6 Notre Dame Fighting Irish in the Cotton Bowl during the 1970 title season?
   a) 53,000
   b) 63,000
   c) 73,000
   d) 83,000

QUESTION 97: Even though the Longhorns won the 1969 National championship, they entered the 1970 season ranked #2 behind what team?
  a) Oklahoma
  b) Ohio State
  c) USC
  d) Alabama

QUESTION 98: What was the halftime score during the 2005 Rose bowl vs. USC?
  a) UT 16-13
  b) USC 21-14
  c) UT 16-10
  d) USC 21-16

QUESTION 99: How many BCS titles has UT won?
  a) 1
  b) 2
  c) 3
  d) 4

QUESTION 100: Prior to Mack Brown taking over as UT's head coach, what school did he *NOT* coach at?
  a) Oklahoma State
  b) North Carolina
  c) Appalachian State
  d) Tulane

QUESTION 101: In what other country did former UT legend Darrell Royal coach?
  a) Germany
  b) Mexico
  c) Italy
  d) Canada

"So what if I'm tired? I can rest when I die."
— Major Applewhite

QUESTION 102: In 2000, Darrell Royal was inducted into what state's Hall of Fame?
   a) Oklahoma
   b) Texas
   c) Kansas
   d) Arkansas

QUESTION 103: What is Mack Brown's annual salary?
   a) Just over $2 million
   b) Just over $3 million
   c) Just over $4 million
   d) Just over $5 million

QUESTION 104: Who is the only coach in UT history to record over 200 wins?
   a) Darrell Royal
   b) Mack Brown
   c) Fred Akers
   d) Blair Cherry

QUESTION 105: Where was Mack Brown born?
   a) Oklahoma
   b) North Carolina
   c) Tennessee
   d) North Dakota

QUESTION 106: In what year was the Red River Shootout changed to Red River Rivalry?
   a) 2003
   b) 2004

c) 2005
d) 2006

QUESTION 107: UT's Stadium was originally dedicated to the Texas veteran's that fought in what war?
a) World War I
b) World War II
c) Korean
d) Vietnam

QUESTION 108: In what year was the stadium rededicated to include Texas vets who fought in all wars?
a) 1976
b) 1977
c) 1978
d) 1979

QUESTION 109: What is Colt McCoy's birth name?
a) Richard
b) David
c) Daniel
d) Samuel

QUESTION 110: In 1995, the *Austin American-Statesman* chose an All-time University of Texas football team. Who did they choose as the team's Full Back?
a) Jeff Ward
b) Earl Campbell
c) Steve Worster
d) Roy Williams

QUESTION 111: Going in to the 2010 season, how many victories had the Longhorns recorded?
a) 800
b) 825
c) 850
d) 875

QUESTION 112: On what day did UT play its first sanctioned game in 1893, a game at Dallas U that the Longhorns won 18-16?
   a) Oct. 15
   b) Oct. 30
   c) Nov. 15
   d) Nov. 30

QUESTION 113: Going in to the 2011 season, what is the only school that has more overall wins than Texas?
   a) Michigan
   b) Ohio State
   c) Alabama
   d) Notre Dame

QUESTION 114: You must be in the _____ grade or lower to participate in the Longhorns Kids Club.
   a) Ninth
   b) Eighth
   c) Seventh
   d) Sixth

QUESTION 115: What was Texas' final ranking in the first AP Poll in 1936?
   a) Not Ranked
   b) 3rd
   c) 5th
   d) 7th

QUESTION 116: UT recorded its _____ win in the 1970 Cotton bowl?
   a) 425th
   b) 450th
   c) 475th
   d) 500th

QUESTION 117: In what year did UT play its first Thanksgiving Day game, a 38-0 win over San Antonio?
- a) 1890
- b) 1895
- c) 1900
- d) 1905

QUESTION 118: Who did the Longhorns beat in their first Thanksgiving Day game at Memorial Stadium during the 1924 season, a 7-0 UT win?
- a) Baylor
- b) Texas Tech
- c) Texas A&M
- d) Rice

QUESTION 119: Going in to the 2011 campaign, how many times has a Mack Brown team lost only one game during the season?
- a) 1
- b) 2
- c) 3
- d) 4

QUESTION 120: In 1998 vs. Oklahoma, Major Applewhite threw a 97 yard touchdown pass, the longest scoring pass in UT history, to what receiver?
- a) Roy Williams
- b) Wane McGarity
- c) Victor Ike
- d) Ricky Williams

QUESTION 121: Although it wasn't the first "official" game recorded by UT, the school actually played a non- sanctioned game against a local Austin high school team in 1883. What high school did the Longhorns play?
- a) Lanier
- b) Reagan

c) Bickler
d) Westlake

QUESTION 122: Because of the challenge of cleaning white uniforms after a football game in 1897, UT wore these colors for three years. What colors did the Longhorns wear from 1897-1900?
a) Orange and Maroon
b) Orange and Blue
c) Blue and Yellow
d) Yellow and Green

QUESTION 123: On the official 2010 UT Football schedule poster, what is the main focus of the photo?
a) The BCS Crystal Ball Trophy
b) A football helmet
c) Mack Brown
d) The football field

QUESTION 124: The Texas Longhorns retired Colt McCoy's jersey. What number did they retire?
a) 10
b) 11
c) 12
d) 13

QUESTION 125: Colt McCoy was selected as the _____ overall selection in the 2010 NFL draft by the Cleveland Browns?
a) 65th
b) 75th
c) 85th
d) 95th

QUESTION 126: Through the 2010 season, how many Big 12 South Division titles do the Longhorns have?
a) 4
b) 5

c) 6
d) 7

QUESTION 127: Through the 2010 season, the Longhorns have never lost to a member of what Conference?
a) Mountain West Conference
b) Western Athletic Conference
c) Conference USA

QUESTION 128: Through the 2010 season, how many years have the Longhorns won at least ten games?
a) 23
b) 24
c) 25
d) 26

QUESTION 129: From 2000-2010, the Longhorns held the NCAA record for most consecutive weeks ranked in the Top 25. How many weeks were the Longhorns ranked?
a) 160
b) 162
c) 164
d) 166

QUESTION 130: How many Bowl games have the Longhorns tied through the 2010 season?
a) 1
b) 2
c) 3
d) 4

QUESTION 131: What is the official website of Texas Football?
a) http://www.mackbrown-texasfootball.com
b) http://www.utfootball.com
c) http://www. texasfootball.com
d) http://www.utgridiron.com

QUESTION 132: What Longhorn Senior did *NOT* play in the 2011 Under Armour Senior Bowl?
a) Sam Acho
b) Quan Cosby
c) Curtis Brown

QUESTION 133: During the 2011 season, what coach was *NOT* a co-offensive coordinator?
a) Bryan Harsin
b) Major Applewhite
c) Jerry Gray

QUESTION 134: How many seasons did former Texas great Jerry Gray spend in the NFL as a player or coach?
a) 11
b) 18
c) 23
d) 30

QUESTION 135: Who was the only Longhorn drafted in the first round of the 2010 NFL draft?
a) Colt McCoy
b) Sergio Kindle
c) Lamar Houston
d) Earl Thomas

QUESTION 136: In 1938 Hugh Wolfe became the first Longhorn drafted by an NFL team. What team drafted him?
a) Brooklyn Tigers
b) Pittsburgh Steelers
c) New York Giants
d) Philadelphia Eagles

QUESTION 137: In what year did the NFL draft 17 Texas Longhorns?
a) 1984
b) 1986

c) 1988
d) 1990

QUESTION 138: Who was the first UT Longhorn to play in the NFL's Pro Bowl? Hint: he played on the 1942 Chicago Bears.
a) Bobby Layne
b) George Sauer
c) Bill Hughes
d) Nathan Vasher

QUESTION 139: What former Longhorn was a member of the Pittsburgh Steelers 2006 Super Bowl team?
a) Casey Hampton
b) Marcus Tubbs
c) D.D. Lewis

QUESTION 140: How many Longhorns played in the '88 Super Bowl between the Redskins and the Broncos?
a) 4
b) 5
c) 6
d) 7

QUESTION 141: Where was former UT Defensive Coordinator Will Muschamp a Graduate Assistant?
a) LSU
b) Georgia
c) Auburn
d) Miami

QUESTION 142: Where did current Defensive Coordinator Manny Diaz earn his Bachelor's degree in Communications?
a) Florida
b) Miami
c) South Florida
d) Florida State

QUESTION 143: How many NFL players has Strength and Conditioning Coach Jeff Madden worked with?
- a) Under 50
- b) 100
- c) 150
- d) Over 200

QUESTION 144: What team does the UT faithful HEX each year?
- a) Oklahoma
- b) Texas A&M
- c) Texas Tech
- d) Baylor

QUESTION 145: The Texas Alma Mater was written in 1903 by _____?
- a) John Smith
- b) John Sinclair
- c) John Brown
- d) John Silverman

QUESTION 146: Where does the original "Eyes of Texas" hang?
- a) Old Main
- b) Burdine Hall
- c) Alumni Center
- d) North Office Building

QUESTION 147: Has Texas ever beat Harvard Football?
- a) Yes
- b) No

QUESTION 148: When was the last time Texas played Florida?
- a) 1940
- b) 1960
- c) 1980
- d) 2000

QUESTION 149: In 1951, Texas had one game televised. Who was their opponent?
a) Texas A&M
b) Oklahoma
c) SMU
d) TCU

QUESTION 150: In what year did UT play their last Home game on Astroturf?
a) 1993
b) 1994
c) 1995

QUESTION 151: While playing in Austin, what jersey number did Ricky Williams *NOT* wear?
a) 11
b) 33
c) 34
d) 37

QUESTION 152: Where was the last Southwest Conference title game played; a 16-6 UT win?
a) Austin
b) Dallas
c) Lubbock
d) College Station

QUESTION 153: Besides the No. 1 lighting up the Tower for a National title, what was the last number, besides 1 to charm it up?
a) 12
b) 33
c) 34
d) 42

"If you want to surf, move to Hawaii. If you like to shop, move to New York. If you like acting and Hollywood, move to California. But if you like college football, move to Texas."
— *Ricky Williams*

QUESTION 154: In 2001, it had been ____ years since UT had won a Bowl game outside the great state of Texas.
a) 15
b) 30
c) 40
d) 50

QUESTION 155: Who founded the Longhorn band?
a) J.K. Davidson
b) E.P. Schoch
c) B.E. Voo
d) M. Alanis

QUESTION 156: On its way to a National title in 1983, what team beat them in the Cotton Bowl to squash those title hopes?
a) LSU
b) Georgia
c) Auburn
d) Washington

QUESTION 157: What former UT All-American and coach led the Longhorns to a Southwest Conference title?
a) David McWilliams
b) Colt McCoy

c) Major Applewhite
d) Harley Clark

QUESTION 158: Who is the UT playing field named after?
a) Wayne McGarity
b) Darryl K. Royal
c) Joe Jamail
d) Mack Brown

QUESTION 159: What was Mack Brown's record during his first season in Austin?
a) 7-5
b) 8-4
c) 9-3
d) 9-4

QUESTION 160: During the East-West Shrine game in 2011, senior tight end Greg Smith led all receivers with how many yards?
a) 57
b) 67
c) 77
d) 87

QUESTION 161: How many ex-Longhorns were selected to play in the 2011 NFL Pro Bowl?
a) 3
b) 4
c) 5
d) 6

QUESTION 162: Who was UT's opponent in the 1984 Freedom Bowl?
a) Michigan
b) UCLA
c) Iowa
d) North Carolina

QUESTION 163: In the 2007 Holiday Bowl, Texas put a beating on Arizona State. What was the final score?
   a) 52-34
   b) 61-21
   c) 43-12
   d) 34-0

QUESTION 164: As of 2010, what Big 12 team has as many bowl wins as Texas has ties in Bowl games?
   a) Iowa State
   b) Kansas
   c) Kansas State
   d) Baylor

QUESTION 165: How many stadium suites are housed in the Reese M. Rowling Hall, located on the east side of DKR-Texas Memorial Stadium?
   a) 58
   b) 60
   c) 62
   d) 64

QUESTION 166: What former UT Longhorn holds the school record for most rushing yards in a game as a freshman with 213 yards?
   a) Jamaal Benson
   b) Vince Young
   c) Ricky Williams
   d) Cedric Benson

QUESTION 167: What former UT All-American holds the Texas individual Bowl game record for rushing attempts with 30 runs?
   a) Ricky Williams
   b) Major Applewhite
   c) Vince Young

QUESTION 168: What former Longhorn holds the record for most receiving yards in an individual Bowl game with 242 yards?
   a) Jordan Shipley
   b) Tony Jones
   c) Quan Cosby
   d) Bobby Layne

QUESTION 169: How many points did UT score vs. LSU in the 1963 Cotton Bowl?
   a) 0
   b) 7
   c) 14
   d) 21

QUESTION 170: During the 2009 Fiesta Bowl, UT set a school record for most first downs in a single Bowl game. How many first downs did the Longhorns convert?
   a) 32
   b) 33
   c) 34
   d) 35

QUESTION 171: During the 2010 season, how many rushing TDs did starting QB Garrett Gilbert score?
   a) 5
   b) 6
   c) 7
   d) 8

QUESTION 172: Who graced the Sports Illustrated cover on January 9, 2006?
   a) Mack Brown
   b) Bevo
   c) Colt McCoy
   d) Vince Young

QUESTION 173: On the cover of the October 20, 2008 edition of Sports Illustrated, Colt McCoy is making a move on the defense of what school?
   a) Oklahoma State
   b) Oklahoma
   c) Baylor
   d) Texas Tech

QUESTION 174: What Texas Longhorn graced the cover of the December 15, 1969 cover of Sports Illustrated?
   a) Earl Campbell
   b) James Street
   c) John Hughes
   d) Cardell Williams

QUESTION 175: Going into the 2011 season, how many UT Football Letter Winners have a last name that starts with a Z?
   a) 3
   b) 4
   c) 5
   d) 6

QUESTION 176: When did Case McCoy enroll at UT?
   a) January 2010
   b) August 2010
   c) June 2010
   d) May 2010

QUESTION 177: What former UT standout intercepted 4 passes in a single game?
   a) Bill Bradley, 1968
   b) Earl Thomas, 2009
   c) Noble Doss, 1939
   d) Nathan Vasher, 2003

QUESTION 178: What former UT star has the most interceptions returned for TDs in a career, with 4?

a) Rod Babers
b) Greg Brown
c) Michael Huff
d) Alan Lowry

QUESTION 179: What UT defensive standout recorded 499 career tackles?
a) Tony Degrate, 1984
b) Lionel Johnson, 1976
c) Rick Fenlaw, 1975
d) Brett Hager, 1988

QUESTION 180: During the 1998 season, the Longhorns averaged _____ in attendance during their 6 home games?
a) 76,542
b) 77,440
c) 82, 673
d) 83,333

QUESTION 181: What UT player won the 2010 Danny Wuerffel trophy, which represents academics, athletics, community service and character?
a) Sam Acho
b) Chet Moss
c) Nate Jones
d) Cedric Griffin

QUESTION 182: What former Longhorn won the 2010 Ed Block Courage award?
a) James Street
b) Cedric Griffin
c) Bill Bradley
d) Earl Campbell

QUESTION 183: In what year was the name The University of

Texas officially changed to The University of Texas at Austin?
   a) 1967
   b) 1968
   c) 1969
   d) 1970

QUESTION 184: True or False: Bevo I was served as the main course at a UT football banquet?
   a) True
   b) False

QUESTION 185: True or False: Through 2010, Texas has had at least one player selected in each of the NFL drafts dating back to 1938?
   a) True
   b) False

QUESTION 186: Going into the 2011 season, UT has appeared in how many pre-season polls since 1950?
   a) 48
   b) 49
   c) 50
   d) 51

QUESTION 187: Going into the 2011 season, Texas has been ranked in the Top 10 of the AP Poll a total of ____ weeks?
   a) 422
   b) 425
   c) 433
   d) 436

QUESTION 188: Going in to the 2011 campaign, UT has won 10 or more games _____ times?
   a) 20
   b) 21
   c) 22
   d) 23

QUESTION 189: In what year was Texas ranked 17th in the final Coaches poll, but was not ranked in the final AP poll?
a) 1959
b) 1960
c) 1961
d) 1972

QUESTION 190: What year was Texas ranked 2nd in the final AP and Coaches poll?
a) 1963
b) 1968
c) 2005
d) 2009

QUESTION 191: During the 1963 National Championship season, what AP ranking did UT open the season with?
a) 3rd
b) 4th
c) 5th
d) 6th

QUESTION 192: During the 1969 National Championship season, what AP ranking did UT open the season with?
a) 3rd
b) 4th
c) 5th
d) 6th

QUESTION 193: Which player listed was one of the Captain's on the 1970 National championship team?
a) Scott Henderson
b) Jim Morris
c) Bill Catlett
d) Scott Moore

QUESTION 194: In what year did former Longhorn star Earl

Campbell play his last NFL season?
   a) 1984
   b) 1985
   c) 1986
   d) 1987

QUESTION 195: How many all-purpose yards did Ricky Williams collect during his career in Austin?
   a) 6,986
   b) 7,107
   c) 7,206
   d) 7,342

QUESTION 196: During Earl Campbell's freshman season in 1974, how many touchdowns did he score?
   a) 2
   b) 4
   c) 6
   d) 8

QUESTION 197: What UT Longhorn won the 2007 Draddy Trophy, which awards the top scholar-football player in the nation?
   a) Colt McCoy
   b) Dallas Griffin
   c) Sam Acho

QUESTION 198: What former Texas coach was hired as the University of Florida Head Coach after the departure of Urban Meyer?
   a) Dan Quinn
   b) Aubrey Hill
   c) Bryant Young
   d) Will Muschamp

QUESTION 199: Which player was not a Captain on the 2009

UT team?
- a) Jordan Shipley
- b) Colt McCoy
- c) Sergio Kindle
- d) Roy Miller

QUESTION 200: Who did UT play in their first game of the 2011 season?
- a) Rice
- b) BYU
- c) UCLA
- d) Iowa State

Texas Longhorns IQ
Answer Key

___ **QUESTION 1:** B

___ **QUESTION 2:** B

___ **QUESTION 3:** C

___ **QUESTION 4:** D

___ **QUESTION 5:** D

___ **QUESTION 6:** A

___ **QUESTION 7:** D

___ **QUESTION 8:** C

___ **QUESTION 9:** C

___ **QUESTION 10:** A

___ **QUESTION 11:** D

___ **QUESTION 12:** D

___ **QUESTION 13:** A

___ **QUESTION 14:** B

___ **QUESTION 15:** B

___ **QUESTION 16:** C

___ **QUESTION 17:** A

___ **QUESTION 18:** B

___ **QUESTION 19:** C

___ **QUESTION 20:** B

___ **QUESTION 21:** A

___ **QUESTION 22:** B

___ **QUESTION 23:** C

___ **QUESTION 24:** B

___ **QUESTION 25:** B

___ **QUESTION 26:** C

___ **QUESTION 27:** D

___ **QUESTION 28:** C

___ **QUESTION 29:** A

___ **QUESTION 30:** B

___ **QUESTION 31:** C

___ **QUESTION 32:** C

___ **QUESTION 33:** D

___ **QUESTION 34:** A

___ **QUESTION 35:** B

___ **QUESTION 36:** A

___ **QUESTION 37:** C

___ **QUESTION 38:** A

___ **QUESTION 39:** A

___ **QUESTION 40:** C

___ **QUESTION 41:** A

___ **QUESTION 42:** A

___ **QUESTION 43:** D

___ **QUESTION 44:** C

___ **QUESTION 45:** B

___ **QUESTION 46:** B

___ **QUESTION 47:** A

___ **QUESTION 48:** C

___ **QUESTION 49:** D

___ **QUESTION 50:** B

___ **QUESTION 51:** B

___ **QUESTION 52:** D

___ **QUESTION 53:** C

___ **QUESTION 54:** D

___ **QUESTION 55:** A

___ **QUESTION 56:** B

___ **QUESTION 57:** D

___ **QUESTION 58:** D

___ **QUESTION 59:** B

___ **QUESTION 60:** C

___ **QUESTION 61:** C

___ **QUESTION 62:** C

___ **QUESTION 63:** B

___ **QUESTION 64:** D

___ **QUESTION 65:** B

___ **QUESTION 66:** B

___ **QUESTION 67:** D

___ **QUESTION 68:** B

___ **QUESTION 69:** A

___ **QUESTION 70:** B

___ **QUESTION 71:** B

___ **QUESTION 72:** C

___ **QUESTION 73:** B

___ **QUESTION 74:** A

___ **QUESTION 75:** C

___ **QUESTION 76:** C

___ **QUESTION 77:** A

___ **QUESTION 78:** D

___ **QUESTION 79:** B

___ **QUESTION 80:** D

___ **QUESTION 81:** B

___ **QUESTION 82:** D

___ **QUESTION 83:** B

___ **QUESTION 84:** C

___ **QUESTION 85:** C

___ **QUESTION 86:** D

___ **QUESTION 87:** B

___ **QUESTION 88:** C

___ **QUESTION 89:** C

___ **QUESTION 90:** C

___ **QUESTION 91:** A

___ **QUESTION 92:** D

___ **QUESTION 93:** B

___ **QUESTION 94:** C

___ **QUESTION 95:** C

___ **QUESTION 96:** C

___ **QUESTION 97:** B

___ **QUESTION 98:** C

___ **QUESTION 99:** A

___ **QUESTION 100:** A

___ **QUESTION 101:** D

___ **QUESTION 102:** A

___ **QUESTION 103:** D

___ **QUESTION 104:** B

___ **QUESTION 105:** C

___ **QUESTION 106:** C

___ **QUESTION 107:** A

___ **QUESTION 108:** B

___ **QUESTION 109:** C

___ **QUESTION 110:** C

___ **QUESTION 111:** C

___ **QUESTION 112:** D

___ **QUESTION 113:** A

___ **QUESTION 114:** B

___ **QUESTION 115:** A

___ **QUESTION 116:** D

___ **QUESTION 117:** B

___ **QUESTION 118:** C

___ **QUESTION 119:** C

___ **QUESTION 120:** B

___ **QUESTION 121:** C

___ **QUESTION 122:** A

___ **QUESTION 123:** B

___ **QUESTION 124:** C

___ **QUESTION 125:** C

___ **QUESTION 126:** D

___ **QUESTION 127:** B

___ **QUESTION 128:** A

___ **QUESTION 129:** B

___ **QUESTION 130:** B

___ **QUESTION 131:** A

___ **QUESTION 132:** B

___ **QUESTION 133:** C

___ **QUESTION 134:** C

___ **QUESTION 135:** D

___ **QUESTION 136:** B

___ **QUESTION 137:** A

___ **QUESTION 138:** C

___ **QUESTION 139:** A

___ **QUESTION 140:** C

___ **QUESTION 141:** C

___ **QUESTION 142:** D

___ **QUESTION 143:** D

___ **QUESTION 144:** B

___ **QUESTION 145:** B

___ **QUESTION 146:** C

___ **QUESTION 147:** B

___ **QUESTION 148:** A

___ **QUESTION 149:** B

___ **QUESTION 150:** C

___ **QUESTION 151:** B

___ **QUESTION 152:** D

___ **QUESTION 153:** C

___ **QUESTION 154:** D

___ **QUESTION 155:** B

___ **QUESTION 156:** B

___ **QUESTION 157:** A

___ **QUESTION 158:** C

___ **QUESTION 159:** C

___ **QUESTION 160:** C

___ **QUESTION 161:** B

___ **QUESTION 162:** C

___ **QUESTION 163:** A

___ **QUESTION 164:** A

___ **QUESTION 165:** C

___ **QUESTION 166:** D

___ **QUESTION 167:** A

___ **QUESTION 168:** B

___ **QUESTION 169:** A

___ **QUESTION 170:** B

___ **QUESTION 171:** A

___ **QUESTION 172:** D

___ **QUESTION 173:** B

___ **QUESTION 174:** B

___ **QUESTION 175:** C

___ **QUESTION 176:** A

___ **QUESTION 177:** A

___ **QUESTION 178:** C

___ **QUESTION 179:** D

___ **QUESTION 180:** B

___ **QUESTION 181:** A

___ **QUESTION 182:** B

___ **QUESTION 183:** A

___ **QUESTION 184:** A

___ **QUESTION 185:** A

___ **QUESTION 186:** C

___ **QUESTION 187:** D

___ **QUESTION 188:** D

___ **QUESTION 189:** B

___ **QUESTION 190:** D

___ **QUESTION 191:** C

___ **QUESTION 192:** B

___ **QUESTION 193:** A

___ **QUESTION 194:** B

___ **QUESTION 195:** C

___ **QUESTION 196:** C

___ **QUESTION 197:** B

___ **QUESTION 198:** D

___ **QUESTION 199:** D

___ **QUESTION 200:** A

Got your total? Here's how your score breaks down:

YOU'RE OFFICIALLY THE LONGHORNS STARTING QB	= 180 – 200
YOU'RE THE LONGHORNS FEATURED RB	= 160 – 179
YOU'RE THE LONGHORNS PRIMARY WR	= 140 – 159
YOU'RE THE BACK-UP TO THE RB WHO BLOCKS	= 120 – 139
I CAN GIVE YOU DIRECTIONS TO AUSTIN	= 119 OR LESS

Think you can do better? Be on the lookout for *Texas Longhorns Trivia IQ, Volume II.*

About the Author

RICHARD BROWN IS a graduate of the University of Texas. A community volunteer, teacher, and writer, Richard currently resides in South Texas. This is his fourth book and first trivia title.

References

- *mackbrown-texasfootball.com*
- *texassports.com*
- *texas.247sports.com*
- *espn.com*
- *Yahoo! Sports*
- *cbssports.com*
- *foxsports.com*

About Black Mesa

BLACK MESA IS a Florida-based publishing company that specializes in sports history and trivia books. Look for these popular titles in our trivia IQ series:

- *Mixed Martial Arts (Volumes I & II)*
- *Boston Red Sox (Volumes I & II)*
- *Tampa Bay Rays*
- *New York Yankees*
- *Atlanta Braves*
- *Major League Baseball*
- *Milwaukee Brewers*
- *St. Louis Cardinals*
- *Boston Celtics*
- *University of Florida Gators Football*
- *University of Georgia Bulldogs Football*
- *University of Texas A&M Aggies Football*
- *University of Oklahoma Sooners Football*
- *New England Patriots*

For information about special discounts for bulk purchases, please email:

black.mesa.publishing@gmail.com

www.blackmesabooks.com

Sports by the Numbers Series

- *Major League Baseball*
- *New York Yankees*
- *Boston Red Sox*
- *San Francisco Giants*
- *University of Oklahoma Football*
- *University of Georgia Football*
- *Penn State University Football*
- *NASCAR*
- *Sacramento Kings Basketball*
- *Mixed Martial Arts*

Available Soon

- *Texas Rangers*
- *Los Angeles Dodgers*
- *Boston Celtics*
- *Dallas Cowboys*